PORTRAIT OF A FILM

PORTRAIT

The Making of *White Nights*

Eve Arnold

Anthony Crickmay

Introduction by

Harry N. Abrams, Inc.,

OF A FILM

Photographs and Texts by

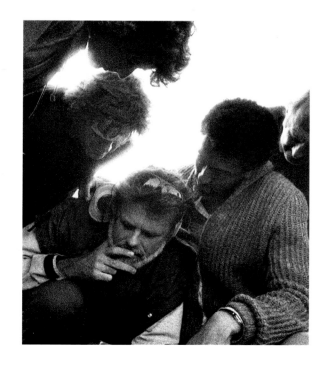

Josef Koudelka

Terry O'Neill

Taylor Hackford

Publishers, New York

Editor: Margaret Donovan

Designer: Dirk Luykx

I'd like to give special thanks to: Guy McElwaine and Columbia Pictures,
who recognized the value of this project and had the guts to step up and make
it happen; Mike Medavoy, with whom I conceived the pairing of Baryshnikov and Hines;
and Allen Burry, whose dedication and tireless energy made this book a reality.
Taylor Hackford

White Nights

COLUMBIA PICTURES PRESENTS
A NEW VISIONS PRODUCTION A TAYLOR HACKFORD FILM
MIKHAIL BARYSHNIKOV · GREGORY HINES
"WHITE NIGHTS"
STARRING GERALDINE PAGE · HELEN MIRREN · JERZY SKOLIMOWSKI
ISABELLA ROSSELLINI MUSIC SCORE BY MICHEL COLOMBIER CHOREOGRAPHY BY TWYLA THARP
SCREENPLAY BY JAMES GOLDMAN AND ERIC HUGHES STORY BY JAMES GOLDMAN
PRODUCED BY TAYLOR HACKFORD AND WILLIAM S. GILMORE DIRECTED BY TAYLOR HACKFORD

Library of Congress Cataloging in Publication Data
Arnold, Eve.
Portrait of a film.
1. White nights (Motion picture) I. White nights
(Motion picture) II. Title.
PN1997.W53373A76 1985   791.43'72   85-6057
ISBN 0-8109-1484-0

The Koudelka essay was written in conjunction with Nan Richardson.

Published in 1985 by Harry N. Abrams, Incorporated, New York
No part of the contents of this book may be reproduced without
the written permission of the publishers.

Printed and bound in Japan

Contents

Introduction

This book came about because I love photographs. There has always been something magical to me about a "still," that specific moment in time captured through a lens. This seemingly real document actually triggers more imaginative energy than the so-called fantasy media of which I am a part. As a feature filmmaker, I have to create a fictional world credible and compelling enough to transport the viewer into a state of suspended reality, to create a vicarious involvement in cinematic story and character. Hundreds of professionals are involved with me in this deception, which literally saturates the viewer with details presented on millions of frames of film. The more graphic the presentation (in other words, the less left to the imagination), the more highly thought of the work. Not so with still photographs. No matter how detailed the information in a single frame, there are always innumerable questions left unanswered. A picture may show daylight, but what hour or day or year is it? A city street may be seen, but which street in what city? Or someone may be crying, but what was the emotional situation that led up to that outburst? This is precisely why I love to look at photographs. I let my imagination fill in the missing information, often creating, I'm sure, very different scenarios from what really occurred.

The photographs in this book are not random views from the work of Arnold, Crickmay, O'Neill, and Koudelka. The subject matter is specific and was assigned to these four talented artists by me. I wanted to capture what I knew was going to be an exceptional experience—the making of *White Nights*—and I was fortunate enough to convince Columbia Pictures that such a documentation would be worthwhile.

There is a unique state of mind that occurs during the making of a film. It's accentuated if the schedule is long and the shooting takes place on location, away from the familiarity of home and family. The goal of creating a believable film reality, of taking written characters, constructed sets, special photographic effects, and such, and putting them together into a credible work of art is a major burden for all concerned. Everyone is aware of the fragility of the equation, of the near impossibility of producing a "really good film." So a collective consciousness is born out of necessity. At first the interdependency is undeniable and terrifying. Actors' performances can be indelibly affected not only by the obvious factors—the hair, makeup, costume, and camera departments—but also by countless constantly changing details: where the sound unit places the microphone, when the light-ing gaffer decides to turn on an incredibly hot bank of lights, or even how early an assistant director calls them to work in the morning. Likewise, production people are at the mercy of actors: the designer needs them to move easily through the set or it won't be seen at its best advantage; the lighting cameraman needs them to hit specific spots where the light is perfect or the balance and composition are completely ruined; the property master must teach them to use a specific prop with ease and familiarity or a crucial plot point can be lost.

So if the various participants are sincere about creating something special and lasting, the key element must be collaboration. The collective consciousness at work, fighting and arguing, shaping and molding, is the true definition of the filmmaking process.

For a director this process never stops. You move from one stage of production to the next, from one group of collaborators to another, and each step is incredibly intense. There is never any time to stop and contemplate, no opportunity to step back and look at what's going on around you. With this project I wanted that chance to look, a record, a kind of "visual journal" to capture some of the special moments I sensed were going to happen. And they did.

In 1982, because of the success of my second feature film, *An Officer and a Gentleman*, I was given the opportunity for the first time to initiate my own projects. In other words, studios would give me money to develop original ideas into scripts. My immediate desire was to create an original dance film. I'd begun my career working on musical performance films for TV, and my first feature, *The Idolmaker*, had been a music film, so a move into the more complex genre of dance film was not only a logical step, it was also a long-standing ambition. My interest was not, however, in the traditional "All Singing…All Dancing" variety of Hollywood extravaganza. In fact, I had turned down opportunities to adapt successful Broadway shows to the screen. Although these films are often immensely popular, it's my belief that they are seldom artistically satisfying, because they are translations of performance material designed for another medium. A few, like *Cabaret*, make wonderful films, but most are bastardizations, regardless of how successful they are at the box office. So, if one is going to risk failure, it might as well be on something original and daring.

I set out to develop a unique mixture of dramatic narrative and dance, a realistic film in which dance occurred as a natural outgrowth of the dramatic action. This isn't difficult if the story revolves around a theatrical setting, but, even in successful stage adaptations, performance numbers, regardless of how brilliant, inevitably stop the dramatic flow and bring the narrative to a standstill. I wanted something else: a story not based on performance but still using dance as a tool to drive the dramatic action forward.

This basic premise immediately created several thorny problems. For instance, such a film would first and foremost require accomplished actors who could support a complicated, full-length narrative. It would also demand fine, even brilliant dancers, if it was to contribute memorable dance sequences to a genre already loaded with them. This combination of gifted acting and dancing talent is not easy to come by in Hollywood, where the generalist is king, where the most common casting response is: "No, I don't know how, but I'm sure I can learn it if you give me a couple of weeks." Not in this instance! Some actors can learn to carry themselves like dancers, and certain talented filmmakers can use cinematic trickery to make it seem as if an actor is dancing when it is really a dance double, but no one can fake a truly brilliant dance performance. Obviously, I had to cast the film first with great dancers and then design the narrative around their unique personalities and talents.

There were only two dancers in America I hoped to attract to this project, whose work within very different traditions and styles had earned them reputations as being the best, Mikhail Baryshnikov and Gregory Hines.

The world's greatest ballet dancer and the foremost exponent of improvisational tap might seem, at first, like an odd combination—different personalities/backgrounds/ethnicities/dance styles— but I was convinced that they'd make a winning combination. I've always thought of casting as a human chemistry set, so the teaming of these wonderfully talented opposites was a calculated move to spark high competitive energy, a challenge to each man to match the other's brilliance. I met with them individually and proposed my idea. Neither man knew the other, but they were tremendous fans of each other's work and, to my delight, they were interested in the concept if I could come up with the right story.

While both Misha and Greg had acted in movies, neither had done a true starring role. Since in this project they would have to carry the entire film, I knew we'd have to design characters to accentuate their natural strengths. Luckily, both men possess that unique essence Hollywood calls "star quality."

It's a combination of a strong, charismatic personality and an intensity in the eyes that goes right to the soul.

Baryshnikov's eyes flash with intelligence and charm, but there is also an abiding sadness there. Through all the success and celebrity, there is a hint of melancholy, reflecting, I think, the loneliness of an exile. Obviously Misha had deep feelings about his 1974 defection, and I felt that unlocking some of these emotions would be the key to his performance.

Greg Hines's eyes are deep and soulful, full of wit and experience, but there is anger there, too. After nearly thirty years of professional entertaining, he has only recently attained some of the acclaim and stardom his rich talent has always deserved. The road was not an easy one, and along the way he must have felt some of the pain and frustration of a black man in American society. I was not going to ignore these emotions either.

I discussed my dance/narrative concept with several writers, and James Goldman (*The Lion in Winter*) came up with a wonderful story idea. What would happen to a celebrated Russian ballet star who had defected to the West ten years earlier if his polar-routed 747 had to make an emergency crash landing in Siberia? Since defection is considered a crime in the U.S.S.R., would the Soviet authorities arrest him? Might they try to persuade him to renounce the West and dance again in Russia? What pressure would they employ? And what if a black American who had deserted in protest against the Vietnam war and had been granted asylum in Russia were to be drawn into a plot by the KGB to coerce the dancer to perform again? I loved this idea. It gave us an opportunity to look at the relationship between individual freedom, art, and politics. A serious film, it explored the aftermath of defection from two points of view: a Russian who defected because of his artistic conscience and an American who left his country because of his political conscience. It was hypothetical, not autobiographical, but it drew on the character strengths and personal experiences of both men. It would also allow for dialogue in dance.

I loved it, but what would Hines and Baryshnikov think? What if the story were too touchy for them, too close to sensitive areas? Misha had declined many offers to film the story of his defection. As for Greg, his role as a black American deserter was not an easy one to make sympathetic. But both men are artists, secure in their talent and not afraid of taking risks. They immediately agreed, and we went to work drawing on personal experience to

Eve Arnold

Anthony Crickmay

create their characters: Nikolai (Kolya) Rodchenko and Raymond Greenwood. Three screenwriters (Goldman, Eric Hughes, and Nancy Dowd) and three studios (Orion, Paramount, and Columbia) later, we began production in England on July 23, 1984.

Added to the cast were Isabella Rossellini, herself the daughter of two fine artists, Ingrid Bergman and Roberto Rossellini, playing Darya, Hines's Russian wife; Jerzy Skolimowski, the renowned expatriate Polish film director, playing Chaiko, the KGB colonel; Helen Mirren, the English-born Shakespearean actress who had just won the Best Actress award at Cannes, playing Galina, prima ballerina with the Kirov and Kolya's former lover; and Geraldine Page, the great American actress, playing Anne Wyatt, Kolya's manager. And joining the six principal actors was a supporting cast of Russians, Poles, Czechs, English, Scots, Americans, Finns, Portuguese, and Yugoslavs; an English crew of seventy; and supplementary personnel from the four countries we shot in—England, Scotland, Finland, and Portugal. It was truly an extraordinary group of people, the most diverse and talented I'd ever worked with.

The logistical problems we faced were awesome. Ninety-five percent of the film takes place inside Russia, in Siberia and Leningrad, but obviously we couldn't shoot there. The hypothesis of the script is painfully real. Misha actually doesn't know what would happen if he were to return to his homeland,

and he's not about to risk finding out. Therefore, we had to create a credible modern Russia of our own.

The environments seen in these photographs are a combination of real locations and constructed sets. Lisbon's venerable San Carlos Opera House with its baroque, tiered boxes had many similarities to the inside of the Kirov in Leningrad: even Baryshnikov was impressed. For our Siberian settlement we used the tiny Finnish fishing village of Reposaari, which had been built by Russians in the nineteenth century. Most of its distinctive wooden buildings were still architecturally intact, right down to the sculpted interior of its small workers' theater, where Greg is first seen performing a number from *Porgy and Bess*. Certain sections of Helsinki double nicely for Leningrad, and we filled three sound stages at Elstree Studios at Borehamwood with elaborate Russian interiors, even recreating the apartment Baryshnikov once had in Leningrad and furnishing it with many of his own pictures and possessions. The dance studio that designer Philip Harrison built was particularly impressive. An oversized, two-story space bounded on one side by mirrors, on the other by a series of arched windows looking out onto the Leningrad skyline and topped by a giant stained-glass window, this room gave choreographer Twyla Tharp the space she needed to create a unique fusion of Hines and Baryshnikov's two very distinctive dance styles.

Obviously, there was a veritable pageant of physical and emotional reality happening every minute

Terry O'Neill

Photographs by Gregory Hines

during the shooting of *White Nights*. There'd be no shortage of material for the "visual journal" I wanted, but I wasn't interested in just snapshots. Photographs are only as good as the eye that sees them, and I wanted several extraordinary "eyes" to shoot this collaborative effort. The four photographers presented here are entirely different in style and approach, and that was exactly what I wanted. Why not examine the filmmaking process from four distinct points of view?

Eve Arnold is a warm, intelligent woman who infuses herself so thoroughly into the lives of her subjects that they allow her unprecedented access. The first time I saw her incredibly intimate studies of Marilyn Monroe and Joan Crawford, I was shocked. I couldn't believe that these two glamorous women would allow themselves to be seen in such vulnerable, nonglamorous situations. Obviously, they loved and trusted Eve enormously, and I wanted her probing, revealing eye on *White Nights*.

Anthony Crickmay's dance photographs were well known to me. He is simply the best at capturing those impossible moments of motion, elevation, and intensity that great dancers are capable of. He was everyone's choice to shoot the dance sequences.

Terry O'Neill had not been working as a photographer for some time. He is truly one of the finest "personality specials" in the business, but he had been concentrating on a new career as a film-

maker. With the challenge of working with such a diverse and uniquely talented group of actors, we were able to lure Terry out of retirement.

And, finally, Josef Koudelka was one of my favorite photographers. His magnificent study of European gypsies was to me a milestone of contemporary photography. But although Josef was a member of Magnum, he had assiduously refused to accept any commercial assignments. With few possessions and very little financial security, he embodied the epitome of the uncompromising artist, photographing only what he wanted. Still, I thought I'd propose the project to him and, to my utter amazement, he accepted. This would be his first assignment and he would use the money so that he and the woman he loved could afford to have a baby.

These then were the four artists I chose to make the pictorial record of *White Nights*. Each photographer shot for seven days during production, and there were no suggestions or restrictions as to what they could shoot.

The intensity of the collaboration captured on these pages is a very different reality from what one sees projected on the screen when the film is finished and exhibited. I'm so pleased to be able to share this "other view" of *White Nights* with you. It was the most exhilarating experience of my working life.

Taylor Hackford

Eve Arnold

"Not too glam," the director called to the actress who stood silhouetted by the light coming off the sound stage. The three professionals who surrounded her to check wardrobe, hair, and makeup nodded. It was a familiar refrain, one they heard daily. It was their job to make Isabella Rossellini, one of the world's highest paid models, into a Russian character. Except for a light dusting of powder to keep off the shine and a touch of lip rouge for color there was no makeup. For further authenticity her clothes were a wardrobe mistress's idea of what a Soviet woman in Moscow would wear: a dirndl skirt with horizontal stripes, a cheap cotton shirt, socks and sandals. It had been agreed from the beginning that glamor would be submerged to let the actress emerge.

Now Taylor Hackford, the film's producer/director, came over to check before Isabella went in front of his cameras for the first time. He had done a great deal of planning with her. At the preproduction stage there had been lengthy discussions about her role, and before preliminary rehearsals he had sent her to Russia with Gregory Hines, who plays her husband on screen, to get a sense of the life of the country and the people, to listen to their voices and to develop a rapport with Greg.

It was obvious that the idea had worked. There was an easy camaraderie between them. Also their weeks of rehearsals with the third lead, Mikhail Baryshnikov, had forged a friendship among the three of them. To the photographer watching them it seemed that they were drawn close together by their common situation. Although each had worked before a camera, their careers were peripheral to motion pictures. None had been a full-time actor. Each had been preeminent in his or her chosen field: Baryshnikov in ballet, Hines in tap dancing and musicals, and Rossellini as a television reporter and comedienne in Italy and as an international model. She, in addition, had the burden of having a great deal expected of her because she is the daughter of Ingrid Bergman and Roberto Rossellini. Now they were all taking calculated risks in branching out. They, who had never before had lead roles in a major international Hollywood film, were to carry the responsibility for a motion picture that cost millions.

It was these elements of chance, the Russian roulette so to speak, which intrigued me. The photographer is really a gambler. Every component she works with is variable, from the camera equipment she chooses to the emulsion on the film, from the light source to the expression on the subject's face. It is endlessly changeable and interchangeable,

and the choices (and results) are myriad. In photographing stills on a film set, the practitioner has an additional ingredient to cope with. On set the light is dictated by the lighting cameraman, and thus the photographer's sense of control is further narrowed. Also one must remember that tensions on a film set are generally high. Time is of the essence because costs are of paramount consideration and deadlines must be met. There is little or no extra time for anything except keeping the film quality at peak and getting it done on schedule. Anything that interferes with this is usually given short shrift; the outside photographer coming in has to be on the qui vive where this is concerned and be prepared to make do, to improvise, to look out for every chance opportunity for the unusual picture.

For this kind of unscheduled, seemingly haphazard random whirligig of shooting, it is essential to have done one's homework as far as knowing the background of the film, the cast, and the crew and then to gain the confidence of all the people involved from the clapper loader through the tea lady to the producer and director, to say nothing of the actors. The challenge is high, sometimes (rarely) matched by the sense of accomplishment. It isn't easy, but it can be enormously rewarding. In the case of *White Nights* it was special because the crew was cooperative, the actors marvelous to watch, and Taylor Hackford particularly helpful.

But, and this is a large but, our problems multiplied geometrically because there were four "specials" on this film, each of us expected to present a personal interpretation—Josef Koudelka, his idiosyncratic and highly individual black and white; Terry O'Neill, his technical and personal experience of photographing personalities and movie stars; Anthony Crickmay, his speciality of dance; and I, I suppose, my color and reportage style of photography—all this in a matter of days. Although Allen Burry, the publicist, tried his best to juggle timetables, there were days when the film was top-heavy with stills people. This happened mainly on the days when the principals danced, because it was such a privilege to have a private view in close-up of these two in motion; we all wanted those days.

Although I photographed the dancers, the highlights were for me more in the preparation and the aftermath of the dance. It seems to me that dance might be best photographed in a studio, where a photographer who knows dance can call the shots. To try to do it during performance on a sound stage adds an additional dimension of lunacy to an already heavy load of imponderables.

I had been assigned by European and American magazines to do a picture essay on Isabella, so she became the main focus of my interest. I had seen countless smooth, retouched pictures of her as the Lancôme model in the glossy magazines. Usually she was served up as a glorious, disembodied head, her neck draped in silks or sables (the image photographers call "the John the Baptist shot"). She was not only in the advertisements but on endless magazine covers. The image was of great aloof elegance, but even though all lines were removed what came through was a woman, not a commodity created by the light and shadow of the portraitist and the pencil of the retoucher.

Isabella was open, warm, funny, with a great bubbling laugh, and she had an acute mind. Shy at first and then forthcoming with observations and anecdotes, she had her mother's mouth and her father's personality. She took her work seriously but not herself. All the time we saw each other, during and after the filming, what came through was Swedish reserve and Italian ebullience.

She would tell jokes on herself and send herself up. She talked about the problem of replacing her Italian accent with a Russian one. She worked diligently on her speech with Seva, her Russian coach, and when she felt secure in her delivery she called friends in Italy to dazzle them with her Russian accent. But—and here amusement burst forth, choking her with giggles—she said her friends thought it was the Pope speaking.

The work days with Isabella (on the sound stage in England and on location in Finland) were harmonious until we got to the love scenes; then both she and Gregory, her husband on screen, were suddenly diffident and reluctant about still pictures. It was not surprising. It is a daunting prospect to be expected to take off your clothes to go to bed with a stranger in the glare of Klieg lights, before the probing eye of the wide-screen camera, in front of a crew of strangers.

That is only the beginning. The actors are then expected to create an illusion of tenderness and intimacy that will be utterly believable to the viewer. It was a first for both actors and it presented emotional, technical, and time problems: emotional problems because it was an extremely demanding scene; technical problems because it was to be shot by remote control from outside the tiny bedroom with no one inside but the actors and the director; and time problems because Taylor wanted spontaneity, which meant avoiding doing scenes over and over again.

The presence of the stills photographer created an additional problem to the already fraught situation. Actors are not happy to be identified with the kind of picture that has a way of appearing years later to embarrass them. In context, on film, it is part of the whole and rounds out the characters; as a photo by itself, its meaning depends upon the way it is used and how it is captioned. If used badly and captioned unscrupulously, at best it can misrepresent and at worst it can be damaging. Then there were the physical problems; the bedroom was small, and my photographing might interfere with the actors' concentration.

We had built up mutual trust over the time we had worked together, both at work and off the set, and we arrived at a possible solution. I would be able to shoot during briefing, preparation, and rehearsal, then leave, watch the scene being filmed from the video monitor, and then run in for a few minutes, before the lights were shifted for the next take, to get the stills. My responsibility was to work at speed so as not to interfere with either the work of the crew or the mood of the actors, who would be replaying their love scenes for my camera. Since the scene was intended as a gentle and loving one between man and wife, I tried to keep it that way by showing in the expressions on their faces (and the upper part of the body) affection, concern, and appreciation of each for the other.

With Gregory the photographers shared "f stops" and "zones." He is a dedicated amateur picture taker and very good at it. His was yet another camera on set, and he did his own documentation of the film.

Misha was friendly but more reserved. Every once in a while in Finland one wondered what he was thinking so close to his birthplace, but he seemed relaxed. It was only one day in the hotel where we were all staying that one realized how far he had made his adjustment to the West. He pointed out a group of Russian tourists marching through the lobby. Facing them came a group of men in U.S.S.R. army uniforms. The tourists froze, the uniforms marched past, Misha laughed. We had been watching soldier extras from *White Nights*, our own film. But the tourists were real—and startled— wondering heaven knows what at this sudden show of the military.

One other strong personality who stays in the mind is Twyla Tharp, the choreographer. It was wonderful to see her tense, involved little face watching the dancers from the shadows as they moved through their numbers.

Then there was David Watkin, the lighting cameraman whose low-key dramatic lighting was perfect for the film but which gave the stills people nightmares. It was wonderful to see the dancers (on screen) move in and out of the light, but for stills it created problems that we had to be ingenious enough to either use or to overcome. Film, which is projected, has the advantage of having light shine through transparent material so that low-key lighting has a luminosity about it. But the still photograph is printed on opaque paper, and the dark quality has a tendency to go muddy in color. In black-and-white stills, this kind of illumination can be very dramatic.

Like the film itself—a tin of shadows—impressions remain: Isabella's laughter, Greg's taps and his camera, Misha's intensity and passion in his acting and his dance, and Taylor's utter professionalism.

A sense of long, long days remains. Twelve-hour days of work, which wound up being longer if one considers transport back and forth, and meals— endless meals. A film company, certainly this one, seems to go to work on its stomach. The catering (for 130 people) went like this: tea on arrival, A.M. break, lunch, P.M. break, and late break of a full-scale hot dinner when one worked beyond 6:30 in the evening—which one usually did. And, of course, each department had its own electric kettle, and a "cuppa" (hot tea) was always on the hob.

A film comes together as an instant community with its friendships and antipathies, its daily dose of rumors and gossip, and as suddenly as it mushrooms it ends, leaving behind its memories—in this case, happy ones.

Gregory Hines

Mikhail Baryshnikov

Helen Mirren

Isabella Rossellini

Helen Mirren and Florence Faure

Helen Mirren and Taylor Hackford

Jerzy Skolimowski

Geraldine Page

Taylor Hackford, Producer/Director

David Watkin,
Director of Photography

Twyla Tharp,
Choreographer

Trevor Rutherford, Sound Assistant

Dushko Indjic, Boom Operator

Anthony Crickmay

Ray Corbett, Assistant Director

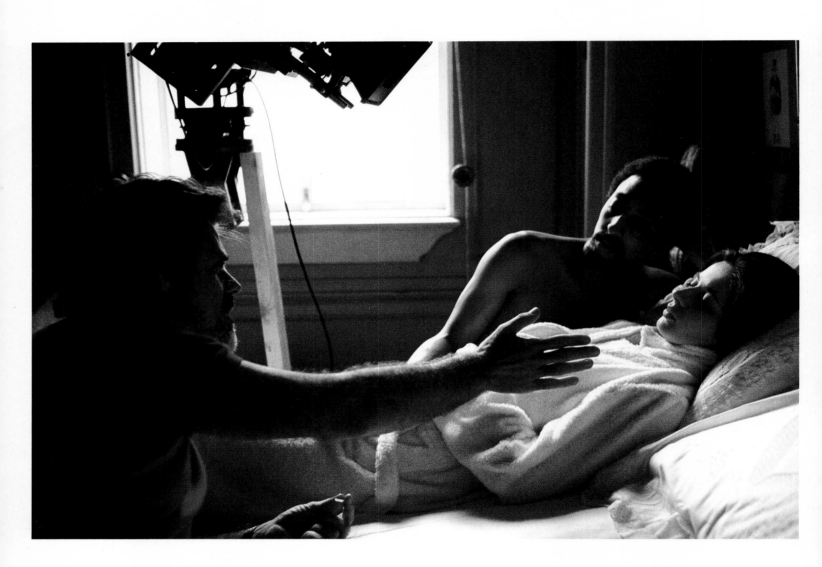

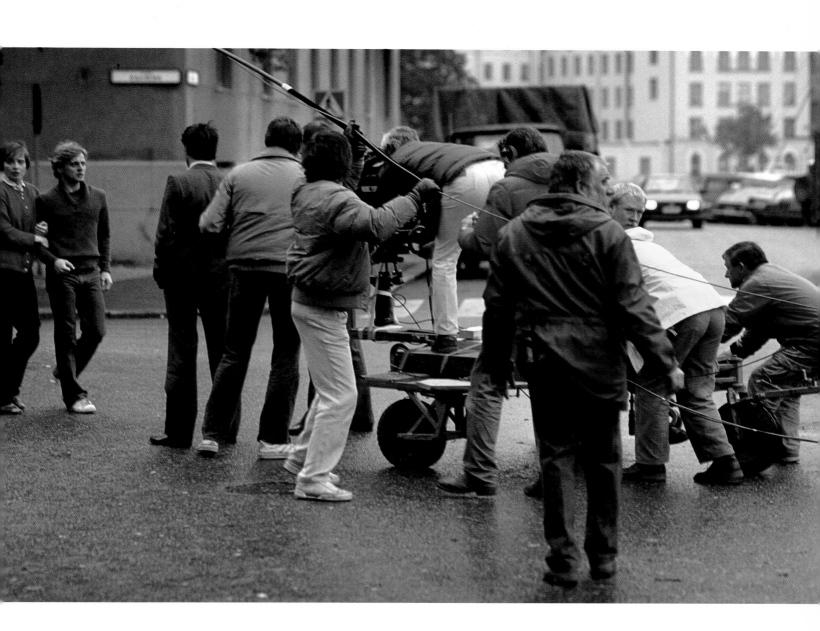

Anthony Crickmay

It has been almost twenty-five years since I began photographing dance. As a result of working for the Royal Opera, I was asked to photograph ballet by Bill Beresford of the Royal Ballet at Covent Garden. My initial reaction was that I did not think I would like it. I knew nothing about dance and had the typical Englishman's view at the time that ballet was a load of old crap about fairies and guys in tights. But Beresford encouraged me to come along, and when I enquired as to exactly what I would be photographing, he replied, "They are Russian, and called the Kirov Ballet from Leningrad." Well, up went the curtain—and instant love affair. It was absolutely mind-blowing seeing those extraordinary people defying laws of gravity and doing things that human bodies were never designed to do. It is a love affair that has never stopped. I still find it as exciting today as then.

You can like photographing ballet on so many different levels. You can admire the purely gymnastic aspect, the actual physical prowess, the musicality, the intellectual content, the decor, scenery, costumes, and artists. I am interested in all of it.

I think possibly there must have been some process whereby, from that first time photographing the Kirov, I felt such a rapport, sympathy, and awe at what dancers do—and I obviously could not be one (wrong shape, too old)—that picture taking became the nearest I could get to doing it myself. Especially if I get dancers into a studio and we create something extraordinary in the way of images. I get almost the same charge out of picture taking as the dancer gets from dancing. It is actually a physical satisfaction for me to capture everything right with the camera.

People are kind enough to say to me that I get that right moment in my pictures. Dancers say that if they are sitting beside me and I am photographing a production I have never seen before I manage to click when the movement is saying the most. Why or how I do it I honestly do not know. I guess it all adds up to my being a frustrated dancer.

To produce the perfect ballet picture you have to start with instinct. When I began shooting the Royal Ballet regularly and had the artists in my studio, I would go to them with my photographs and the dancers would say, this picture could be fine if only he pushed his arm out or if she stretched her leg a bit more. I learned pretty quickly what was classically correct in ballet terms. I guess it is a requirement of a dance photographer to have a certain technical knowledge of ballet, especially for classical dance. You should know the five positions and you have to know what an *attitude* is.

What then happens over the years is that you start to get worried that you are spending too much time getting things classically correct and not enough time on the feeling of dance. It really becomes a difficult marriage, because the positions have to be perfect. If they are not, the pictures cannot be used as publicity shots by the company, which is, after all, paying the bills.

In the past I have had numerous cases of ballet indigestion from trying to get everything perfect and at the same time making sure the picture has life. It was wonderful to venture into advertising and fashion photography because I think now I view ballet with a much freer eye again simply because I do not have an undiluted diet of dance photography.

With the increased interest and development of modern dance, things have changed a lot for me. With modern dance you can be much freer; you can do whatever you like photographically. Feet can be pointed or not as long as the energy and feeling of the dance are there. The kids today do not give a damn whether their feet are stretched, if there is power and life in the picture. Obviously they do not want a positively bad position if they are dancing in a modern ballet that requires them to be very correct with proper arms, stretched feet, and proper placing. Generally, however, it is the feeling of energy and movement in the picture that is more important now.

Classical dance you simply cannot approach in that manner. Even in powerful dramatic ballets such as those Kenneth MacMillan creates you cannot have a dancer's feet all over the place, legs turned in when they are meant to be turned out, arms wild and feet not pointed. Classical dancers spend years and years working at getting their arms in position, backs properly placed, and feet pointed, and when somebody takes a picture where it is all wrong, of course they are upset no matter how exciting the picture might look. All classical dancers look for the smallest detail to be perfect in photographs. Where for me they are in extraordinary positions, legs split, flying through the air, and I say "How about that?" the answer is usually something like, "Oh, that's all right, but look at that left hand." They are trained to look into the mirror and correct every minor fault so that their eye goes immediately to the minutest problem, often failing to notice whether it is overall an exciting picture.

In the case of *White Nights,* the working situation was somewhat different for me. I had never previously worked on a film, although I had photographed plays and ballet performances for television.

The dances created for *White Nights* by Misha,

Greg, and Twyla constitute quite specifically a choreographic telling of the story. If Misha or Greg has a solo or if they dance together, it is a powerful statement. From speaking lines they go directly into a dance, because dance happens to be both their occupations in the film and they use it to say as much as their lines. In the film their faces become as important as their bodies. The photographer must make both work in order for the photograph to be effective. Their faces are speaking volumes; the choreography has been so integrated into the story that it slips from speech to movement with hardly a notice. This does not happen with photographing classical or modern ballet onstage, where it is the dancer's body that means everything.

I had to find an even balance between facial and body expressions in photographing the dance numbers. For instance, during Misha's Vysotsky solo, if he did some sort of spectacular thing that only he can do, like jumping up and down *en pointe* or doing "Baryshnikov" leaps and *attitudes en pointe*, then I clicked, trying to get the best position I could. In spectacular moments, when suddenly he comes sliding forward on his knees with his face pouring passion, obviously to hell with the body position—get the picture. I had to bear in mind all sorts of things while photographing a dance like that and rely heavily on my instincts.

I chose to do *White Nights* because I had not done film before and welcomed the chance to learn something new. Equally important was my enormous respect for Baryshnikov, whom I selected as the cover of one of my books as a token of the high regard I have for him as a performer. Also, Greg Hines happened to be a New York neighbor of mine, and for a long time I wanted to photograph him. I had heard what an extraordinary artist Greg is and discovered in working on *White Nights* how complex, subtle, and imaginative his dancing is. When Greg performs a solo, unlike dancers I had been used to photographing who do the same thing each time, he hardly ever repeats himself. It is an internal conversation he has with himself when he dances. You photograph that with great difficulty. To photograph tap dancing is almost impossible, as I discovered. If you try to stop at any given moment, it can look like nothing.

The sound of the taps is as important as anything else in tap dancing and that cannot be transmitted by a picture. The second problem is that tap dancers on the whole look down and are rather bowed over in comparison to a classical dancer. And it is also difficult to stop tap dancing at a given moment and still get that tremendous feeling of energy into the picture. We got around it as best we could

during a special photographic session whereby Greg and I worked alone together on a prelit stage for three hours. Between us we got the right feeling, and I think we were able to translate that for the stills camera to a much greater extent than if I had just photographed him dancing during the shooting of the film. I could have gotten good results during the filming but in order to obtain the needed amount of good, clear, well-lit photographs I would have had to shoot considerably more than I normally shoot for a classical ballet solo. Watching Greg dance is like listening to a very, very good jazz solo. You get the same complexities and intellectual content from his feet as you do from a jazz musician. How to capture that photographically is a major challenge. There is nothing to avoid, as there is with a classical dancer, but you must find a way of showing his energy and something of what he does.

We started the session with my suggesting something I saw him do during filming. He then suggested a bit and we continued in that vein, building trust and confidence. The fact that I clicked at what we both knew instinctively was the right time led to mutual trust. It is the trust and confidence—when the artist feels he is dealing with somebody who knows what he is trying to do and has an idea of dance—that make for successful dance pictures.

Photographing Misha is very different. For starters he has this famous jump which is always so breathtaking to see, let alone photograph. But mainly he has this absolutely extraordinary placing. If you see him turning (the number of turns he can do without coming down off *demi-pointe* is literally unbelievable as you watch it), you can almost put a line down through the top of his head straight to the floor. His placing within that line is perfect. This contributes to his ease of turning in such a way because he is so centered. Centering is one of the things dancers learn as part of their training. It is why as human beings they tend to come over very "upright" and reserved. With a dancer you have the feeling of meeting somebody who knows who he is and what he is doing, someone who is viewing you from a slight distance.

Misha is a joy to work with in that he is so perfect in some positions it just makes you gasp. You do not have to cheat with photographs of Misha. He gives you everything you want, perfectly placed, as many times as you require.

There were many wonderful experiences on *White Nights*, but one highlight I shall always remember was photographing a rehearsal with Greg and Twyla Tharp. That was one of the most exciting afternoons I have ever spent with two dancers.

Twyla has a remarkable and unique way of dancing herself, and her partnership with Greg produced amazing results. They started out very, very slowly, just warming up in separate areas of the dance studio, practically ignoring each other. Then they graduated to almost doing a ballet together, incorporating all sorts of things. They were trying to outdo each other, racing around the room, fighting. One minute Twyla would be tapping and the next Greg would try and follow her special kind of movement. They just went on like that for several hours. I am passionate about dance and I feel it says an awful lot. Here was something really remarkable: two minds with such different backgrounds really enjoying and communicating with each other. They had such high regard for each other's talent. I knew it was important to try and capture the experience of it all. I had to get fairly decent dance positions of Twyla because she works as hard as any classical ballet dancer to perfect her body. If you are clever there is a way to photograph a dancer in a distorted position as long as it does not make her look like a bad dancer. You must not suggest that she cannot pull it all out straight if she wants to.

Following the session with the two of them, Greg stayed on and danced alone. He made the whole building ring with the sound of the power in those feet. People were coming in off the streets of Lisbon, where we were filming, to find out what the noise was, and dancers from the ballet school we were using crowded in from the other studios to watch. I will never forget the sound he made.

Dancers are used to being told what to do by a choreographer, so most sessions start with suggestions from me. When they come to a photo session they usually tend to go straight to the "center" and wait for developments. Silence while one thinks is never embarrassing for dancers; nor do they ever break into it until you have obviously completed your thought. Once it gets going things develop between you, but just how much depends on the individual artist. Usually, in my own hideous way, I demonstrate what I want them to do. That is the frustrated dancer again, but for me the greatest joy is to have a dancer in my studio. It is like being a kid in a sweet shop not knowing which to choose since they are all so good.

A very special memory was working in the studio with Florence Faure, the young ballerina from Roland Petit's company who was selected to dance *Le Jeune Homme et La Mort* opposite Baryshnikov in the film. Florence had never done a solo session before. She is a very strong technician and a really lovely-looking girl. Very classical face. When I started working with her I had no idea of what sort of dancer she was, so I tested the ground by starting off with color portraits and slowly slithered into dance pictures. First I gave her something to do with the top half of her body. Then the whole body and it became apparent that she was very turned out, had a wonderful back, very high extensions, so we progressed to positions and jumps. Her jump is spectacular. She was not attuned to the camera, but that is just a case of slightly altering the placing. If a dancer is bright and quick to understand, all you do is marginally change the *attitude,* push a knee across a bit more, pull a leg forward, and so on, to flatten the whole thing for a one-plane situation. Of course dancers are used to dancing in a four-dimensional situation where an audience can observe their whole body. It is very hard for them to do a photo session, and they find it extremely strenuous.

For me the greatest difficulty I had with my first movie assignment was learning to shoot around the film cameras. In order to do what I am hired to do, I am used to having the whole stage at my command—lights, dancers, and technicians. This is not possible when you work on a major film like *White Nights* because the film always comes first. Most of the time I had problems with getting where I felt I needed to be. The movie camera was always in that spot. In fact I was very impressed by what director Taylor Hackford did with his camera in relationship to the dance numbers.

When I arrived on the set for the first time, as a dance photographer I had extremely dogmatic views on how dance should be photographed. I right away questioned the camera crew on which lens was being used and could not believe the answer. I discovered they were using a wide-angle lens. That is the worst lens to photograph dancers with from a stills photographer's point of view. It makes the legs look short and the head minuscule if you are above the waist and does the opposite if you are below. Not knowing anything about movies, I thought it sounded unusual, to say the least, and when I found out the camera was going to be placed on the floor most of the time I was totally shocked. Presumably the dancers would end up with feet like giants and tiny pinheads. I was even more amazed when I watched the video playback and saw how brilliantly it worked. I think Taylor found an incredibly interesting and successful way of shooting dance. It is powerful, strong, and very unusual.

White Nights was a memorable experience—at times frustrating and fraught, but enjoyable, invigorating, instructive, and always interesting. And how very privileged to be paid to watch and photograph such supreme artists at work!

Terry O'Neill

I was really hungry to do a good job when the chance came along to work on *White Nights.* At that point in my life I had something to prove to myself and to prove professionally. For the past few years I had pretty much stayed away from photography, preferring to concentrate on launching a career as a film director. When the project I was working on did not materialize, I started to rethink my photographic career, but I wanted to make sure that if I was going to go back to it, the first assignment was the right one. What interests me basically about any job I accept are the people involved. The promise of working with the extraordinary talents taking part in the making of *White Nights* was inspirational and exciting, and I knew it would keep me on my toes every day. I had never photographed dance and when I found out that three other special photographers had been assigned to the picture it became a triple challenge for me.

During the four years I concentrated on directing, I rarely took photographs and I was initially worried that maybe I had become rusty. I did not know if I could still deliver the goods. But I discovered when I actually got going that I was seeing things better, bigger, and more completely than ever before. In a way being apart from the stills camera had become a blessing in disguise: looking through the viewfinder was suddenly really interesting to me again.

Working alongside Eve Arnold, Josef Koudelka, and Anthony Crickmay—three photographers whom I respect tremendously and rate at the top of their fields—was a personal competition for me. I was constantly aware of working with the very best and it made me home in on the assignment even more. I did not want to lag behind and, if there were any lazy traits I had used to get by in the past, I certainly could not afford to employ them on *White Nights.*

Having the others on the same film, and even working on the same day, I think brought out the best in me. On this picture I put my foot on the gas and never took it off. I also felt that if I had a few holes or gaps in my abilities as a photographer, what better way to find out than being surrounded by those three? Having another photographer around facing similar problems gave me somebody else to help find a solution.

I was interested in seeing why we were all chosen and what each of us, shooting the same subject, could contribute in style. I knew I would learn a lot.

Eve Arnold is a unique lady who has inspired the last two generations of photographers. While still maintaining truth and reality, she has a gentleness toward her subjects that makes her very special as a reportage photographer.

To me Anthony Crickmay views the world in terms of dance. No matter what he photographs, there is always a tremendous sense of grace and elegance. His photos have a great understanding of movement, with bodies doing the talking rather than just the faces telling the story. I find his photographs very sensual.

And Josef Koudelka's composition with nature and total concentration on everything going on around him are incredible to me. His mastery of black and white is phenomenal.

I found the whole experience of working with these people exciting, instructive, and a lot of fun. I would love us to work together again sometime. I really miss them.

On a completely different level, having been involved with film directing myself, *White Nights* was interesting for me because I could observe a master talent at work. Taylor Hackford's technical knowledge, determination, decisiveness, positive attitude, and camaraderie with his cast and crew were among the best I have seen. What he did with the actors was exceptional. He coped with the numerous different accents and general lack of screen experience, he filmed dance numbers for the first time, and yet he always maintained a high degree of authenticity. He was fascinating to watch.

My own contribution to *White Nights* was meant to be as a set and studio-session photographer concentrating on capturing the off-camera personalities and relationships of the stars. Except for the studio sessions, I decided to shoot mostly black and white because of the way the film was being presented. The lighting, the sets, the acting all felt very subdued, natural, and almost documentary in flavor. It never seemed technicolor or movieish.

The hard thing about photographing on-set action can be the lighting, as was the case with *White Nights.* The low-key atmosphere brilliantly created by lighting cameraman David Watkin (a genius in his own light) did not make the stills man's job easy. Usually when this happens, I prefer to take the actors away from the set, do my own lighting, and recreate the scene; however, on this film, because of the time factor and the cast and crew's trying to maintain the continuity of the film, it was impossible to remove the actors.

When it came to photographing the dance sequences, there were always two or three film cameras operating, which cut down my chances even more. I had to hit it at a certain time and in a certain place and still stay out of the way of the other cameras. We were not allowed total freedom to move around except in rehearsals, which in some ways worked better but at times had the disadvan-

tage for me of being without music. Before becoming a photographer, I was a modern-jazz drummer and in this case my feel for music allowed me to better anticipate the dynamics of the dance. When the dancers hit their own respective beats, either with their arms, legs, whole bodies, or whatever it took to make a good dance picture, it was always on a precise beat of the music. I am not sure of my results, but because I do love and understand music it made the execution easier.

Another help for me was a brief talk I had with Twyla Tharp. She gave me two very good pieces of advice. First, she told me to get down low because that will help accentuate the whole feeling of movement and give the dancers height. Secondly, to try and stay in a straight line with the dancer, whatever posture or pose he takes. Being totally parallel with them—that was easier said than done, but nevertheless valued guidance. Whatever the outcome of the photographs themselves, a definite highlight of working on *White Nights* was the opportunity to see and enjoy some absolutely world-class dancing.

The studio sessions also provided me with memorable experiences. The difference I find between shooting actors and actresses on set as opposed to in the studio is enormous. Even though they make their living in front of one kind of camera, most actors hate having to go into a studio for posed pictures. They are shy, awkward, and insecure people. On the set there are many people around to distract them, so they are not as conscious of the stills man's presence. They are lost in their characters, and as long as you do not break their concentration it does not seem to be a problem. On set they also have the advantage of working with other actors, so their concentration is not as singular. They feel they are dressing up for their role, presenting a character rather than exposing themselves.

When you go into the studio it is suddenly just the photographer and the person. It is like seeing right into their souls. Unlike the film, which can take up to a year to come out, a photograph can be in your hand that very day. It is immediately indicting. Many celebrities end up being professional posers, but few can feel free enough to let their full personality show through. Technically you end up with perfect pictures, but they are often one dimensional, without much trace of the true nature of the person. What the subjects seldom realize is that they really control the photographer; they think it is the other way around. My job is to get them to react emotionally and then capture it on film. I am totally governed by what they deliver.

I like actors and actresses as people. I feel I can get closer to them in the studio, if it all works, than on the set. I have an understanding and sympathy for what they are trying to do and know how hard it is for them to do it. In a way when I work in a studio it is as close to their reality as people that I can ever get. I look straight into their eyes and under all those artificial circumstances create the most accurate picture of who they are and how they tick. How they appear in front of the stills camera—devoid of all the on-set trappings—is really what they are, what they want to be, and how they would like to be perceived by the world and themselves. That is the reality and I find it fascinating and revealing.

When I do a studio session, the first task is to create the proper atmosphere. I hide in the studio. I try not to be there other than as an extension of the camera. I say very little during the shoot and let the work come from the personality. I gently encourage them when I know it is getting near to what we want, but I find all that stereotyped chat unnecessary and offensive. I try not to break the mood they have established. I respect that it is a struggle for them. I think a good session photographer senses when it is right, and the subject responds to that sense without much dialogue. I just keep moving as fast as I can. It is all about catching isolated moments, and it is up to me to pick those moments as a director selects a close-up or an editor puts together a great piece of film. I have to do it on the spot, in an instant. There is no luxury of time and an editing machine—it has to happen now!

White Nights brought together a great variety of characters. Isabella Rossellini is probably the most extraordinary of all the women I have photographed over the past twenty years in her ability to change moods with great speed for each photograph and still create the perfect picture. A dozen frames on a roll of film are all different and all usable. Working with her explains to me how she has reached the top in her field of fashion and advertising photography, and if she can deliver what she does for stills to the big screen she will be as extraordinary an actress as her mother, Ingrid Bergman.

Mikhail Baryshnikov has a strong personality and he is a natural actor. A successful session with Misha definitely depends on whether or not he wants to have fun. The pictures where he is enjoying himself are far more successful in my opinion. If you go through his photographs you can tell what is on his mind. He does not hide much emotionally.

Gregory Hines is a fascinating person to watch. He is never still for a minute. He is always tapping out intricate rhythms and time changes. It was like being in a room with the Count Basie Orchestra. He would conjure up such wonderful powerhouse dynamics and sounds. In fact, in the jazz vernacular, whenever Greg was around "the joint was jumpin'." He is at the same time quite intense as an actor and really got inside his part. Yet he always made time for a laugh and a joke. Quite a guy, our Greg.

I had photographed Helen Mirren years ago and now she has matured in her ability, like Isabella, to deliver many different moods outside the role she is playing at the moment and to deliver them accurately. She takes time to compose what she is saying and doing, but then that is true of most of the great actresses I have worked with in studio sessions. They approach stills as though they were playing a role, but Helen is confident enough to let her own personality dominate. She is not afraid to expose her feelings. It was Helen who masterminded the session between herself and Misha. She was the motivator and was able to relax and guide him throughout.

When it comes to remembering something special about each of them, it will be Misha's eyes, piercing blue, not unlike Paul Newman's in color, that stay in my mind. I felt they had seen a lot of life and I do not think I ever really got behind them in a photograph.

Gregory has great earnestness to please and was always concerned with being very professional in what he was doing. He also has this terrific sense of humor, which I feel we all caught in our pictures.

Isabella's strange resemblance to her mother fascinates me because I find them totally different physically. I photographed Ingrid Bergman years ago, and she had a completely different bone structure and coloring from her daughter. Yet, when Isabella moves her head slightly in a certain way, you suddenly see this very strong likeness.

Helen has a sensuality that is wonderful to photograph. She is a very, very feminine woman. She also has a lot of class. The combination is a natural.

White Nights, its director, cast, crew, and fellow photographers, left me feeling I had absolutely made the right choice in coming back to photography.

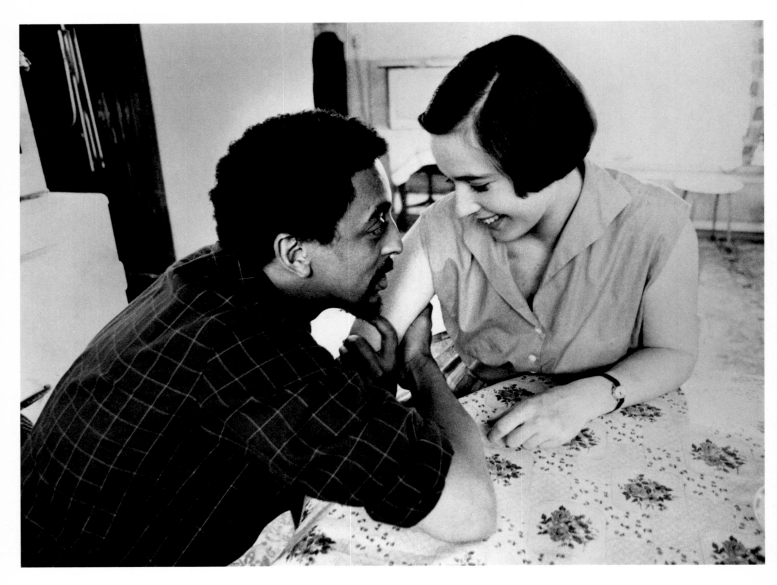

Josef Koudelka

Koudelka does not usually give interviews, prefers not to be quoted. His relationships, even with friends, avoid dwelling on words, even though he is comfortable conversing in five languages. It is a conscious decision; he perceives language as something that runs against mystery, the essence of photography. It is his way of preserving space, of gaining unencumbered freedom for his eye.

His sense of privacy extends to his way of living rough, sleeping on the floors of friends or in the offices of Magnum, eating simply. During the filming of White Nights, Koudelka stayed in a hotel room in England for the first time. With comic bemusement, he tells how the noisy, climate-controlled, hermetically sealed room kept him awake all night as he looked for knobs or buttons to quiet it.

White Nights is the first assignment Josef has ever accepted. Most of his modest income has been earned through the Magnum archive, by the sale of prints, and the subsidy of grants. The decision to work on the film was taken as a result of personal developments in his life: the desire to have a family and the need to provide for them.

Taylor Hackford asked him to come to the set, bring his cameras, and be himself. It was a brave idea to let such a character leap onto the stage of a studio, into a fixed process where entrances and exits, the beginnings and the ends of creative involvement, are as delineated as they are in filmmaking. Koudelka speaks of himself there as a character in the shadows: "I would sit there not taking any pictures. Then, suddenly, I would see something and begin photographing. Some realism in a scene, perhaps, or I do not know what. Taylor would then say, 'If Josef is taking pictures, then something must be going right.'"

Josef also spoke of working with the three main actors in the film. "They were not what I expected," he said, "perhaps because they were not established movie stars. There was no self-consciousness in them." He saw Gregory Hines for the first time in London, a tall, black American loping across the room with a motorized Canon camera swinging around his neck. "'Jesus Christ!' I thought, 'another photographer!' But then he and his wife came up to me and said, 'Can we take your picture?' He was a funny guy."

Koudelka learned about photography through the theater in Prague. There, working with artifice, makeup, light, the stage, night after night, he could take time, reflect, project his thoughts, start over and over again, within the repetition of the stage process. The sense of theater as rehearsal, as visual vocabulary, is still with him. "I was formed by the theater, but I won't go back to it," he said. "I don't want to be a stills photographer. A director from the Comédie Française

offered me work with the company, but I refused—in theater you work on something already finished. Working on this film was an interesting experience for me, but once in my life, if I had the freedom, I would like to take it on as a personal experience, to work on a film from beginning to end, the entire film, even the most boring moments." (The structure of the filming of White Nights made it possible for Koudelka to devote only seven days to the picture.)

Arriving on the set of the small village built by the Russians in Finland before 1910, Josef remarked that working on a film for him was "new—a totally new experience." One day, Baryshnikov was trying to describe the East, Russia, to members of the crew and in frustration turned to him, saying, "You, you know what I mean." Koudelka's photographs of the invasion of Prague were at the time on display in London, and Baryshnikov had seen and felt most strongly about them.

The photographs from White Nights that will last personally for Josef do not come from any script but from some unscripted reality. There is no difference between the way he shoots the stars acting and the crew filming. He recalls that he felt most comfortable photographing during the market sequence, when he was free to move in the open, "There were kids rushing around, a lot of activity." It was natural for him, it was what he liked to do best.

Koudelka says of watching any film that his instinct is to stop it whenever he sees anything strong, to freeze the frame. His belief is in the unique image, not in the building of image with tone, distance, substance, sound, speed, narrative, and continuity. In fact, his insistence on the unique image, and his opposition to the picture essay, are, even for photography, pushed to the extreme. His approach is radically different from the cinematic one.

Josef shoots only in black and white; his world is monochromatic, exclusive of the sensuality of color. He makes photographs based on the abstraction of emotion, on its structure and composition. The portrait of Baryshnikov with a patch above his eye is a picture of a man alone, confronted by the authorities. Although the seven days he worked on this film were so little time in Josef's opinion, the look and feel of these pictures explain what no words can.

Taylor Hackford concludes, "Josef wanted to remain apart while he was working. He wanted a certain objectivity. 'That is as it is,' I said to him. His aloofness was like a protective shield, but by the end of the film, perhaps, it was breaking down. At the wrap party, he came, he drank vodka, he was among the last to leave. He was genuinely liked by all—and he said to me, when it was all over, 'I enjoyed it,' and I think he did."

TAYLOR HACKFORD
JERZY SKOLIMOWSKY
DAVID WATKIN
MIKHAIL BARYSHNIKOV

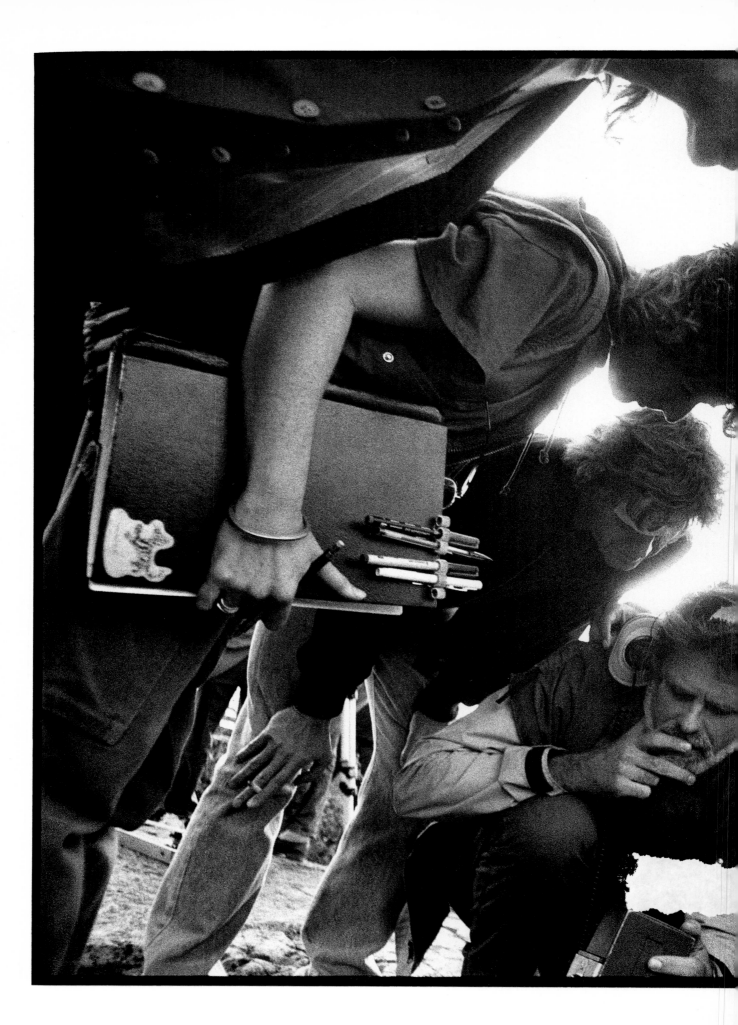